Mandala Art Volume 2

Shelby Lynn

ISBN:9781082232305
ISBN-13:

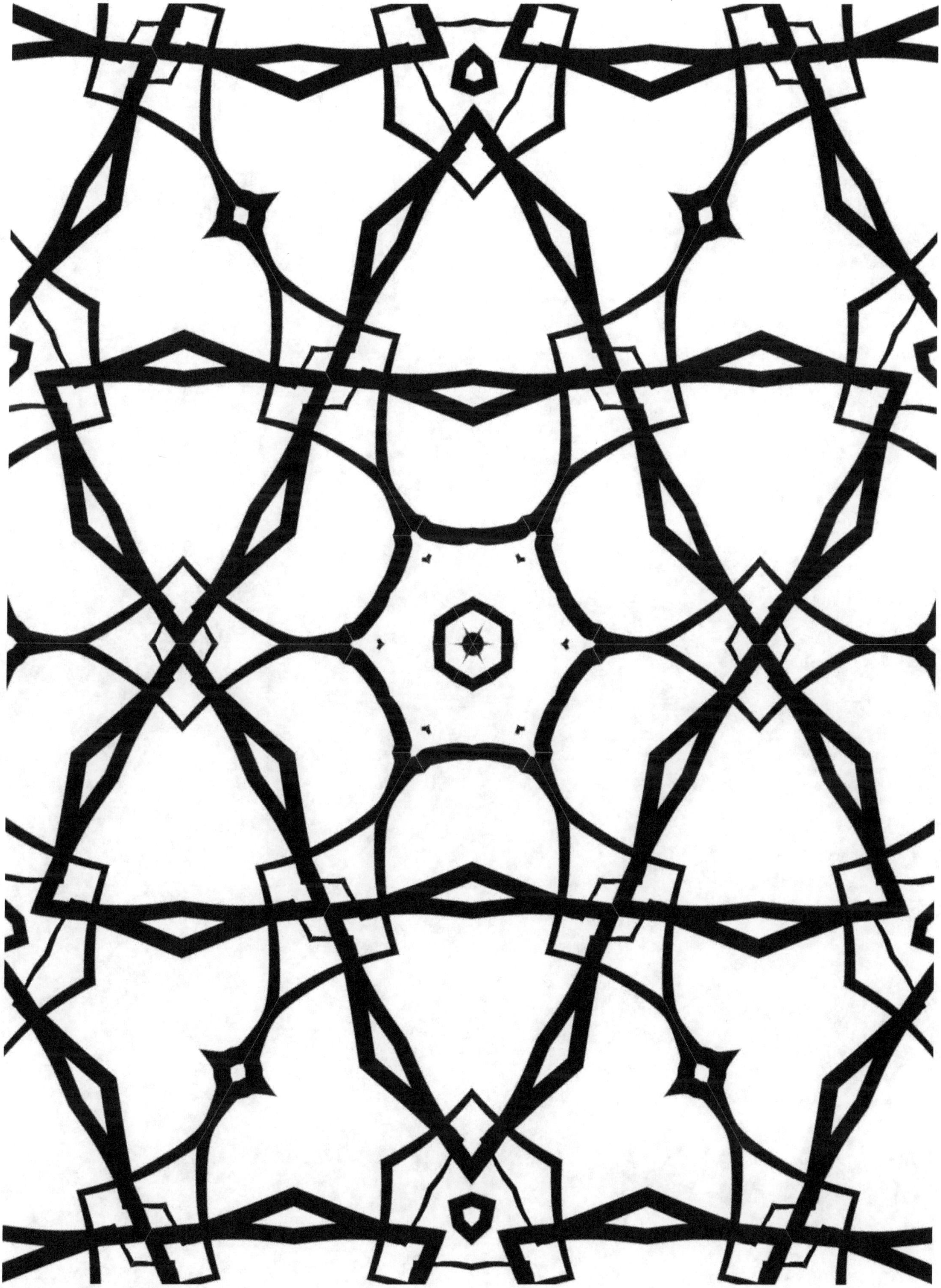

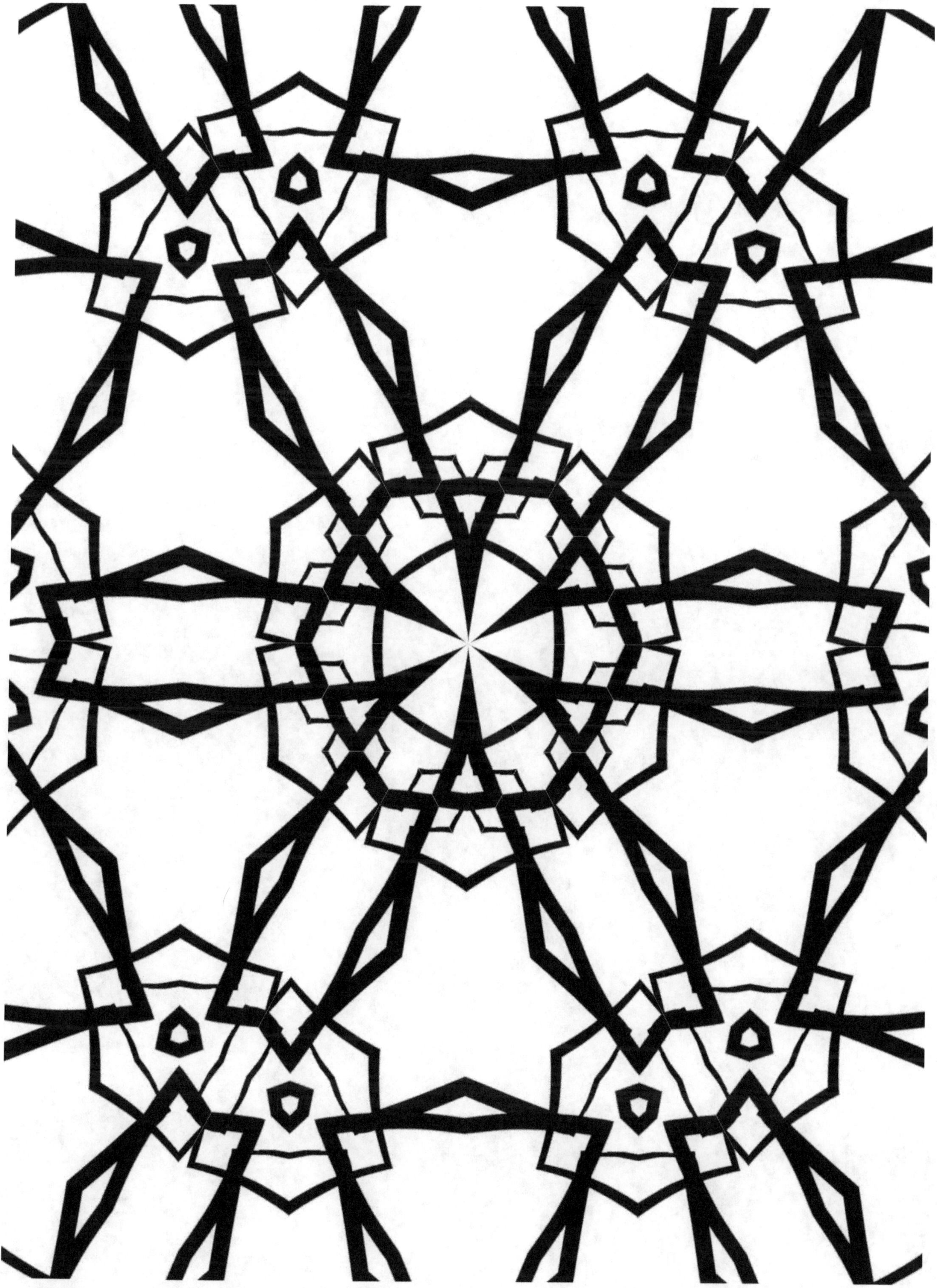

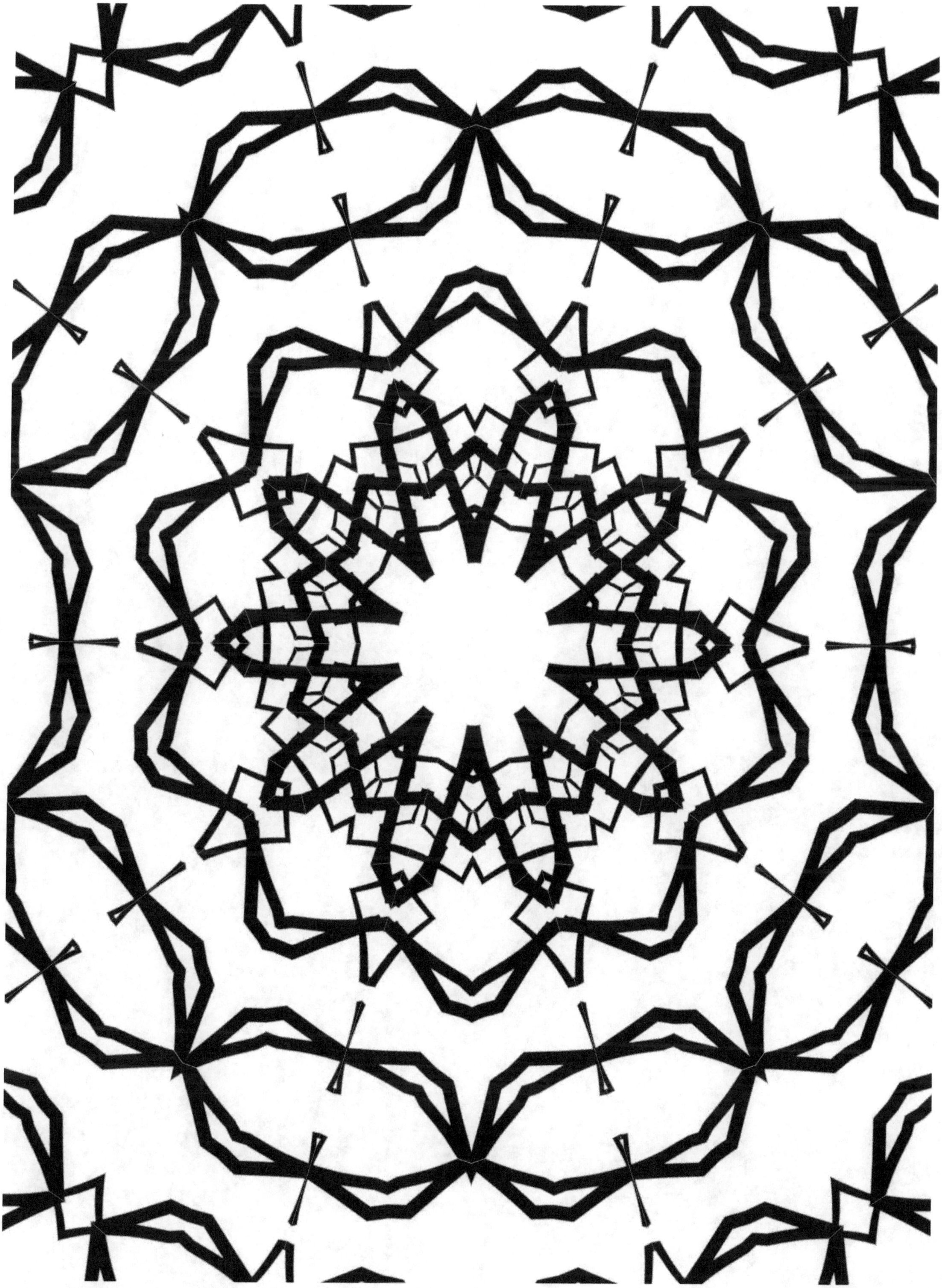

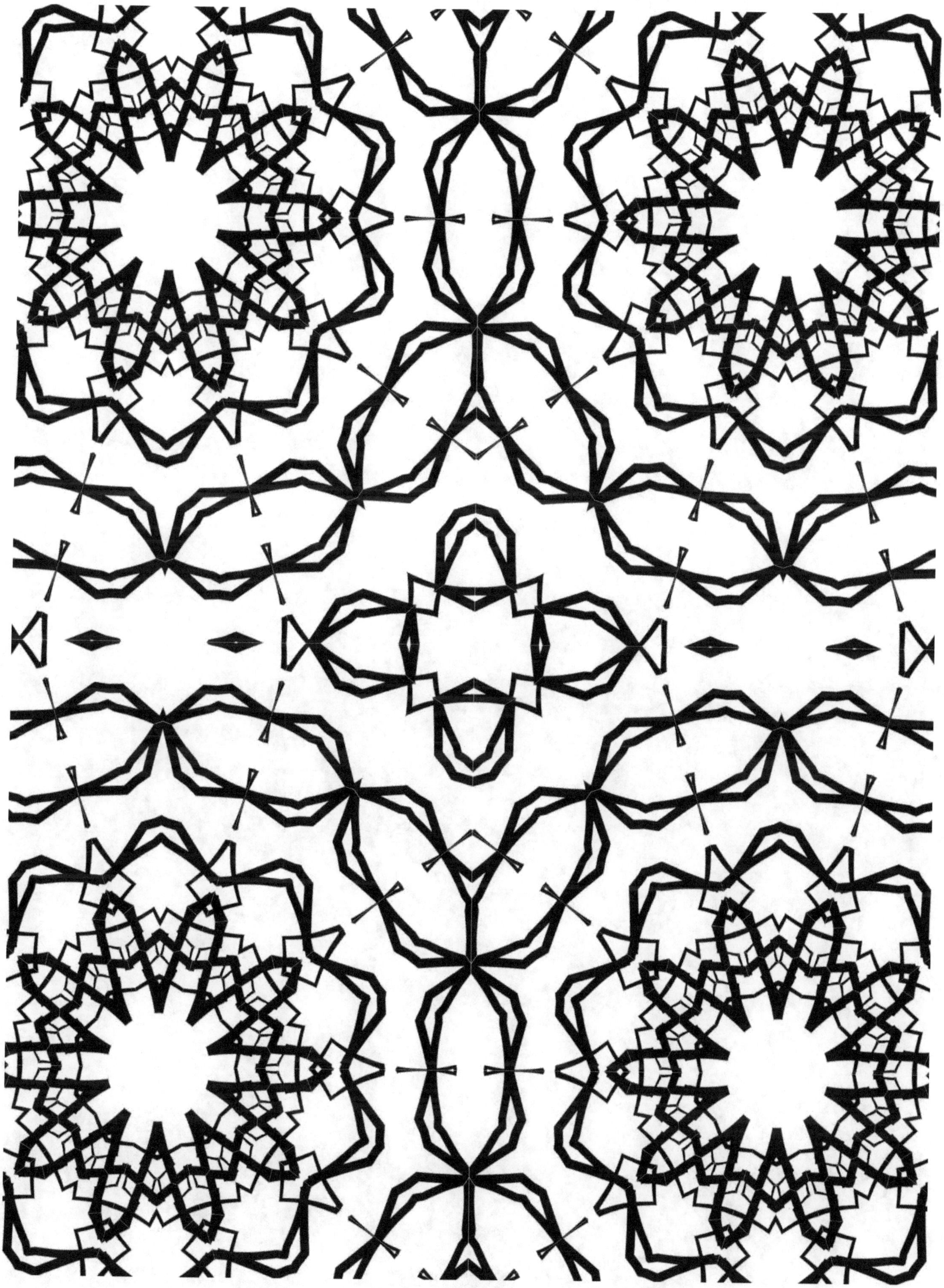

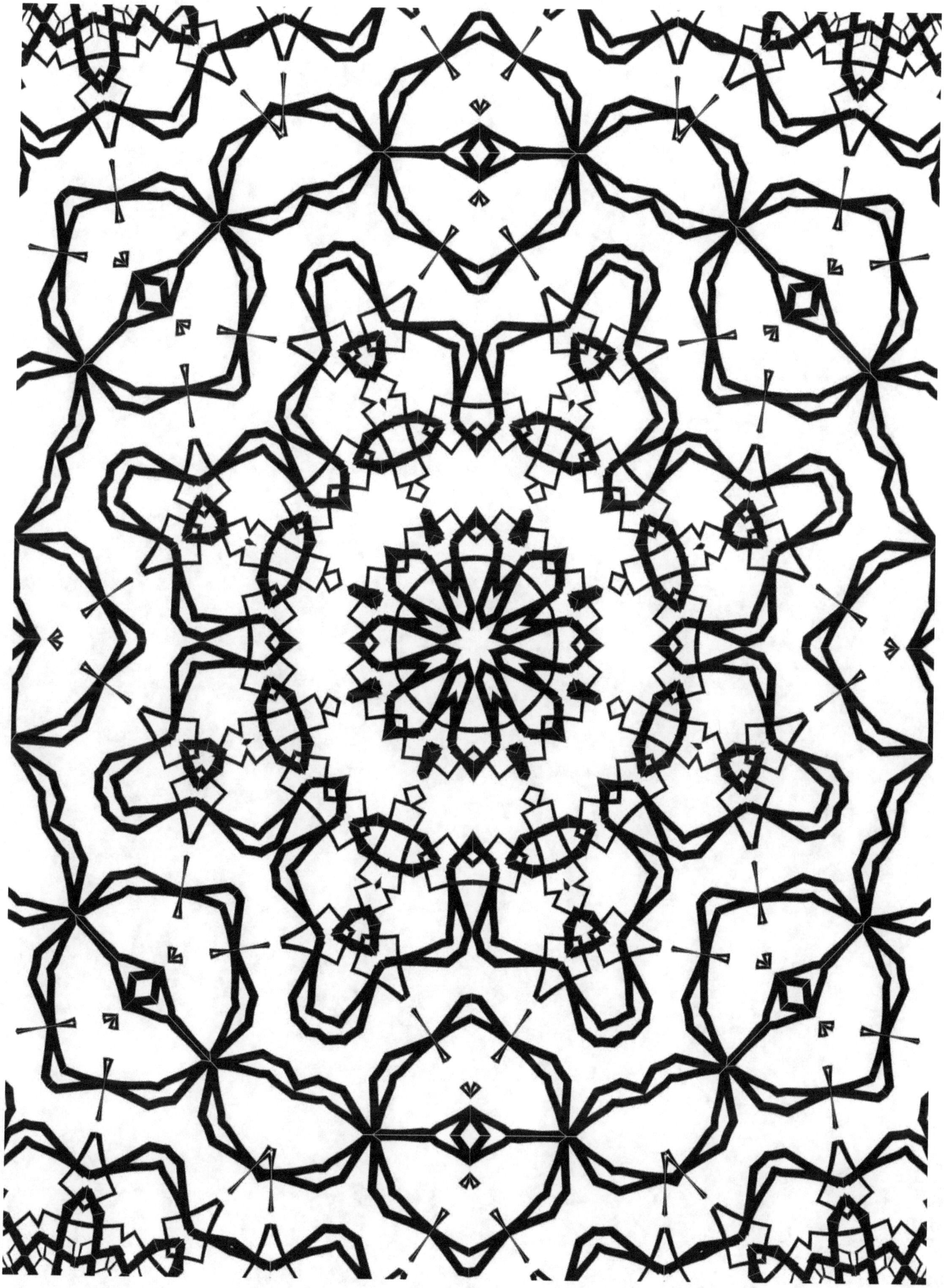

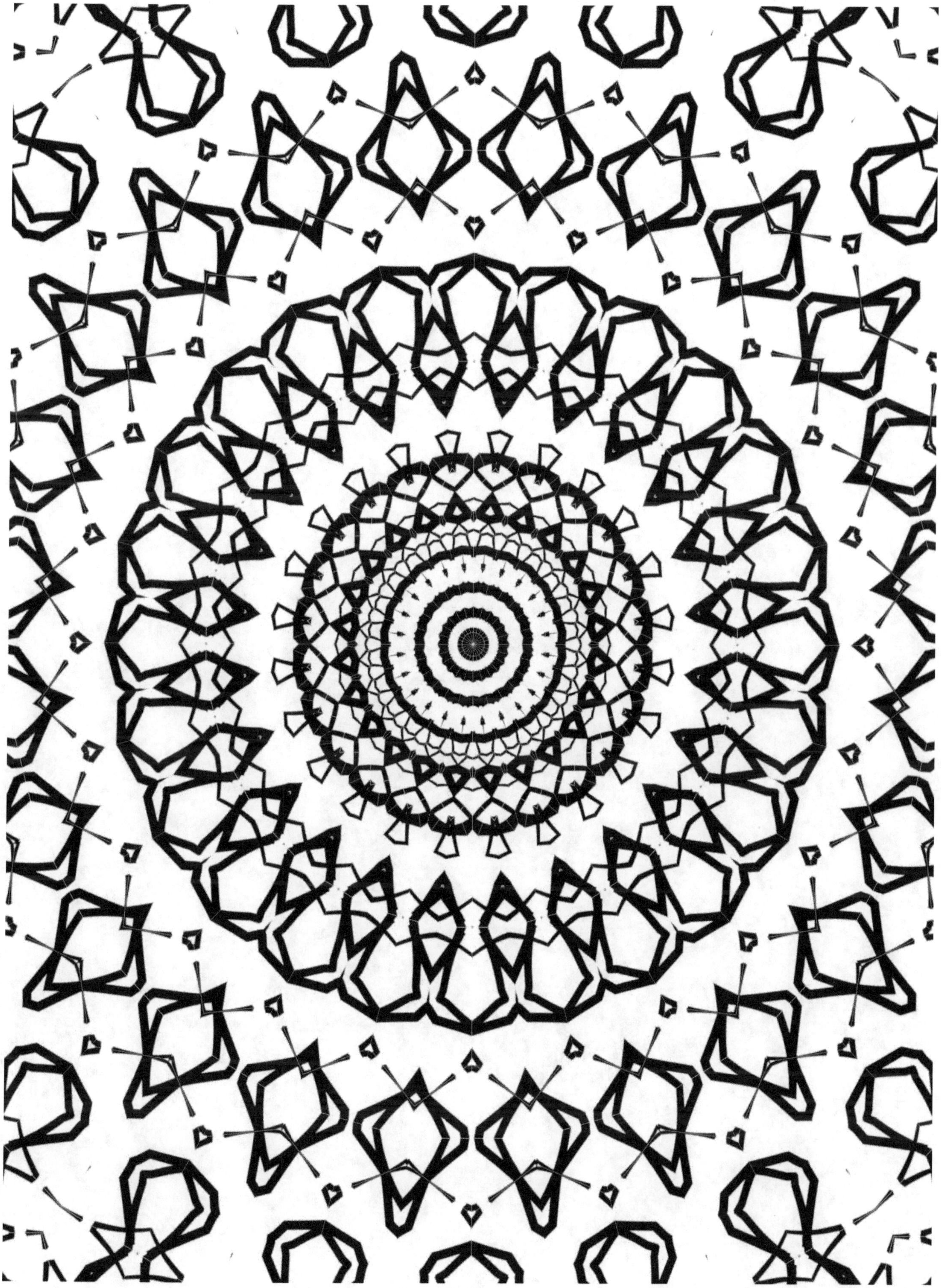

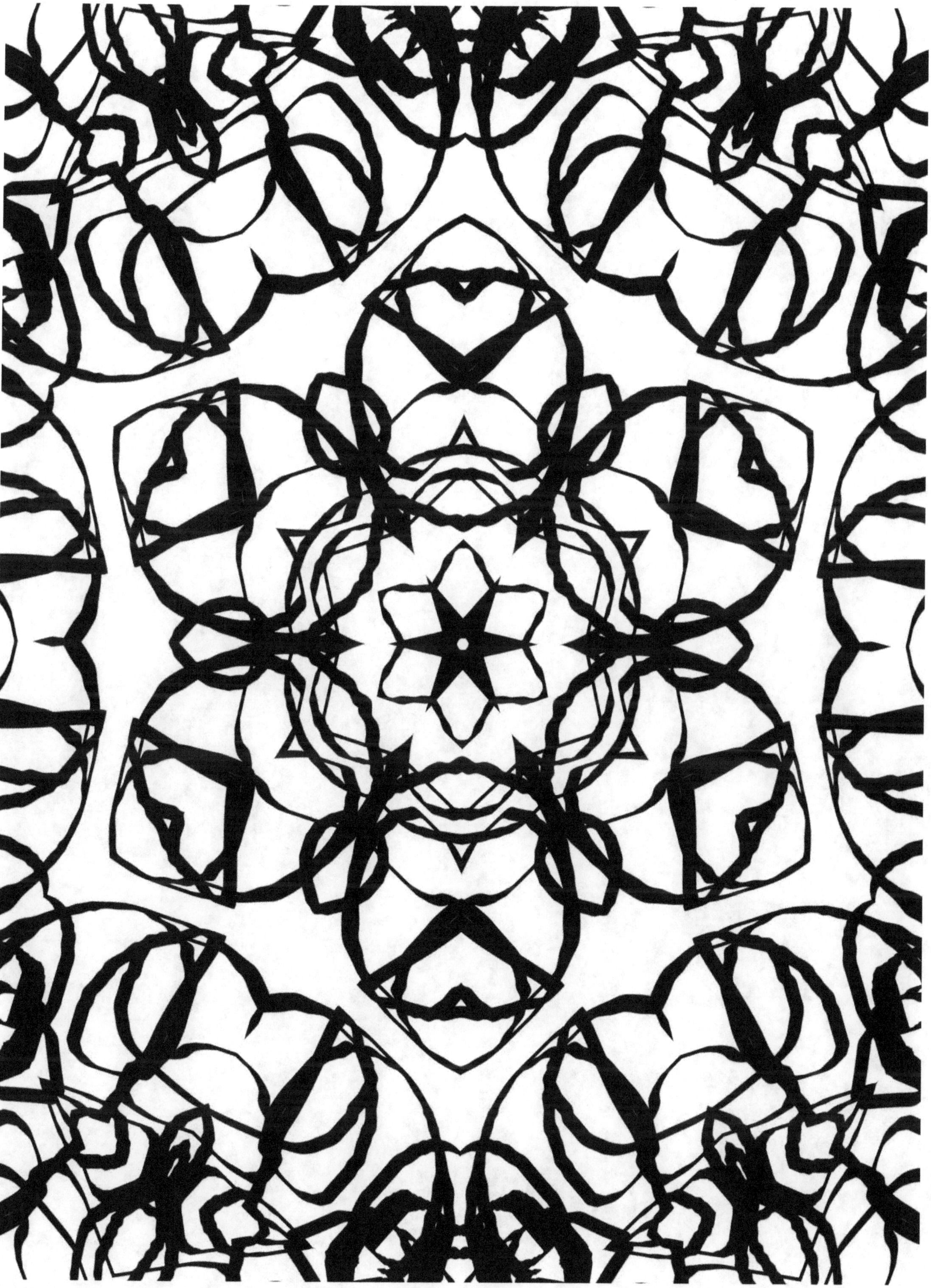

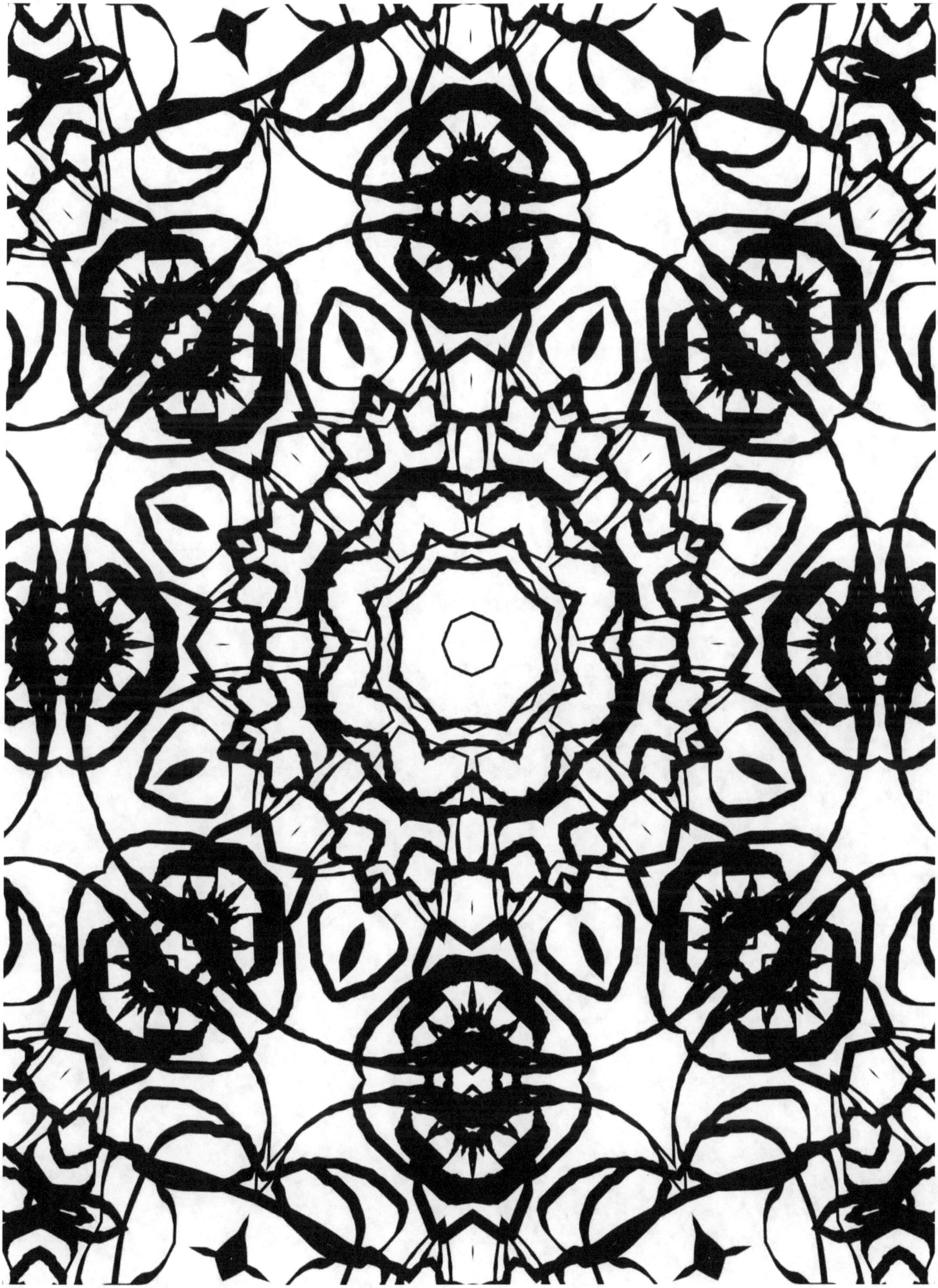

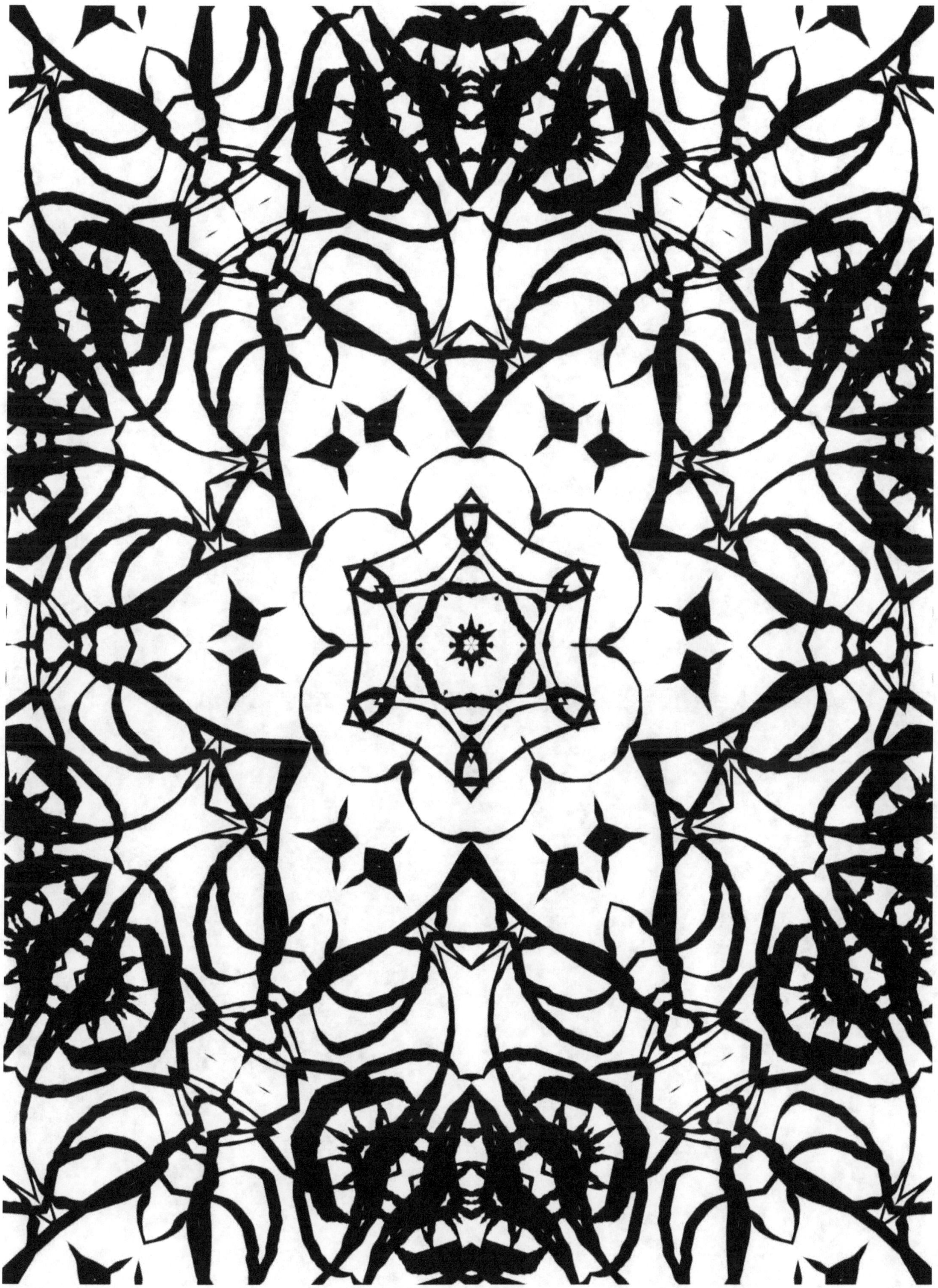

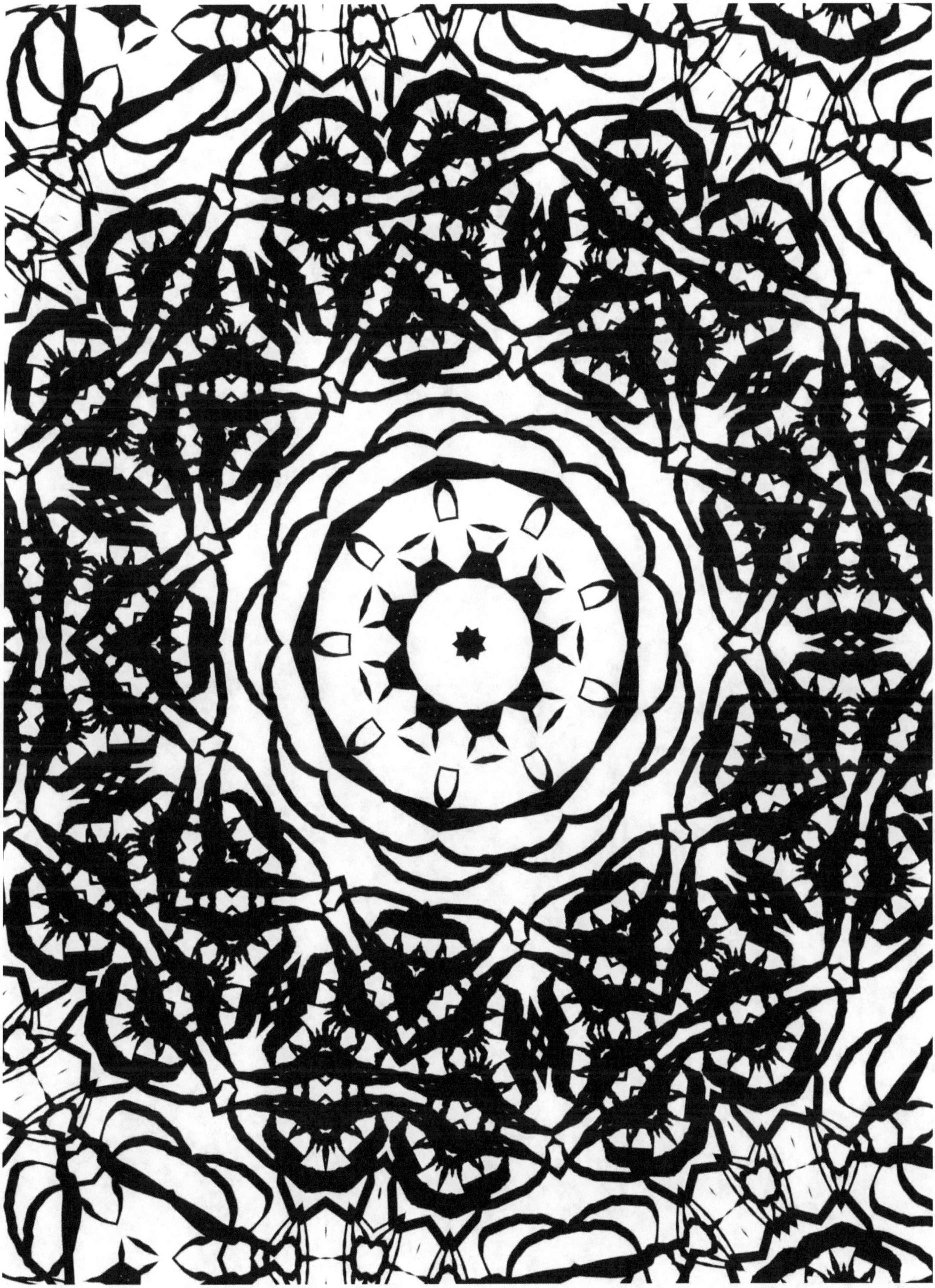

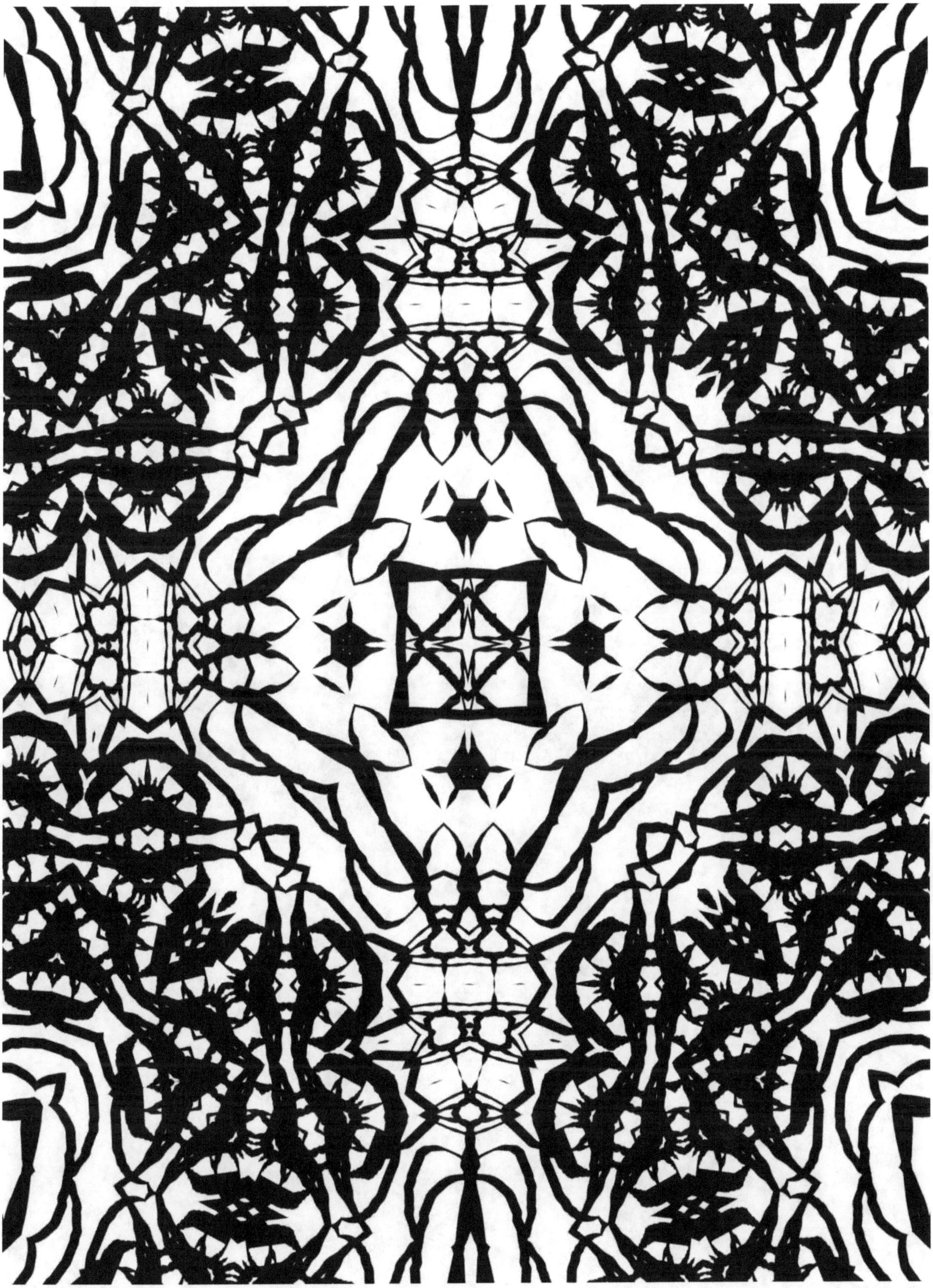

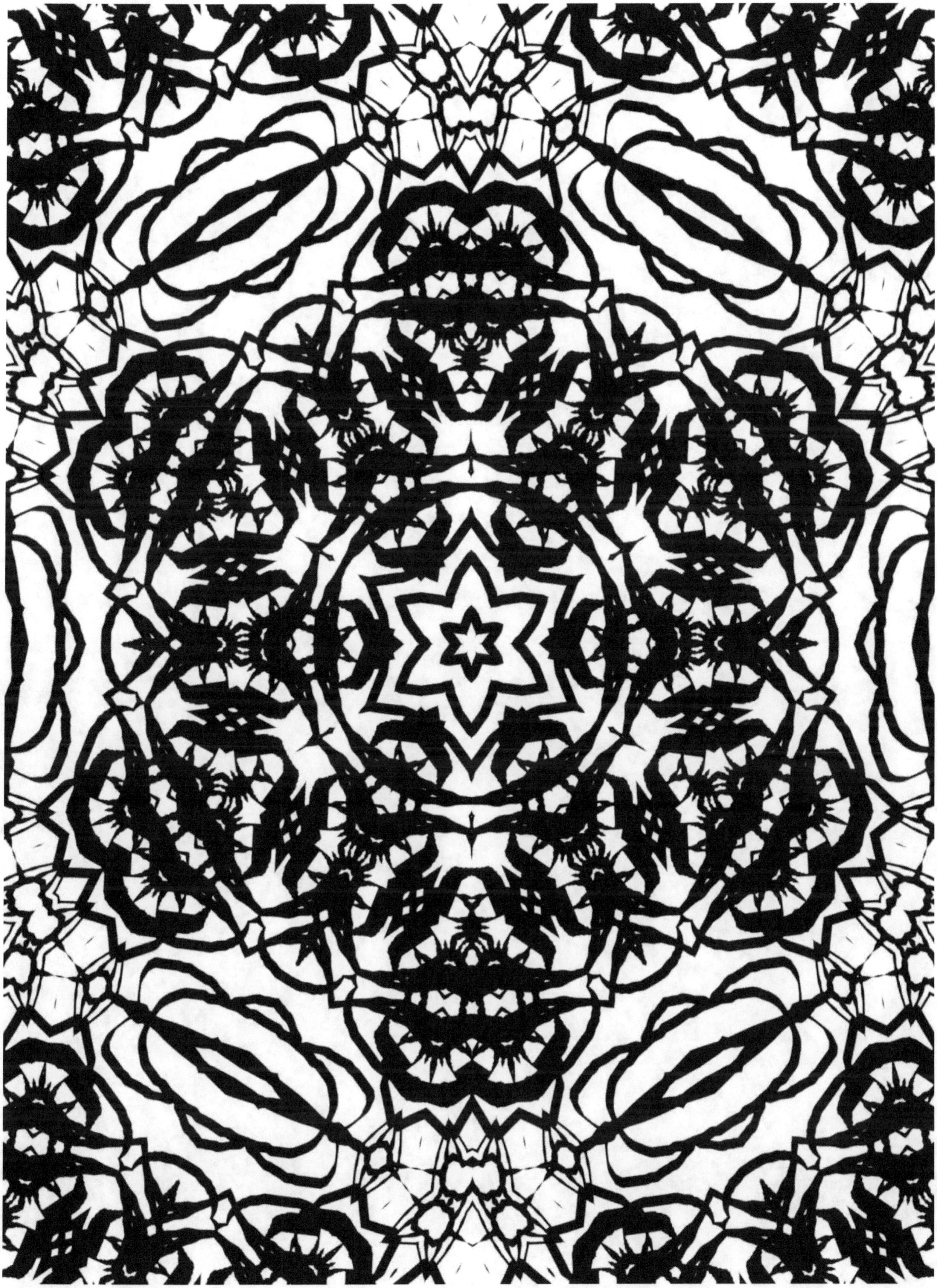

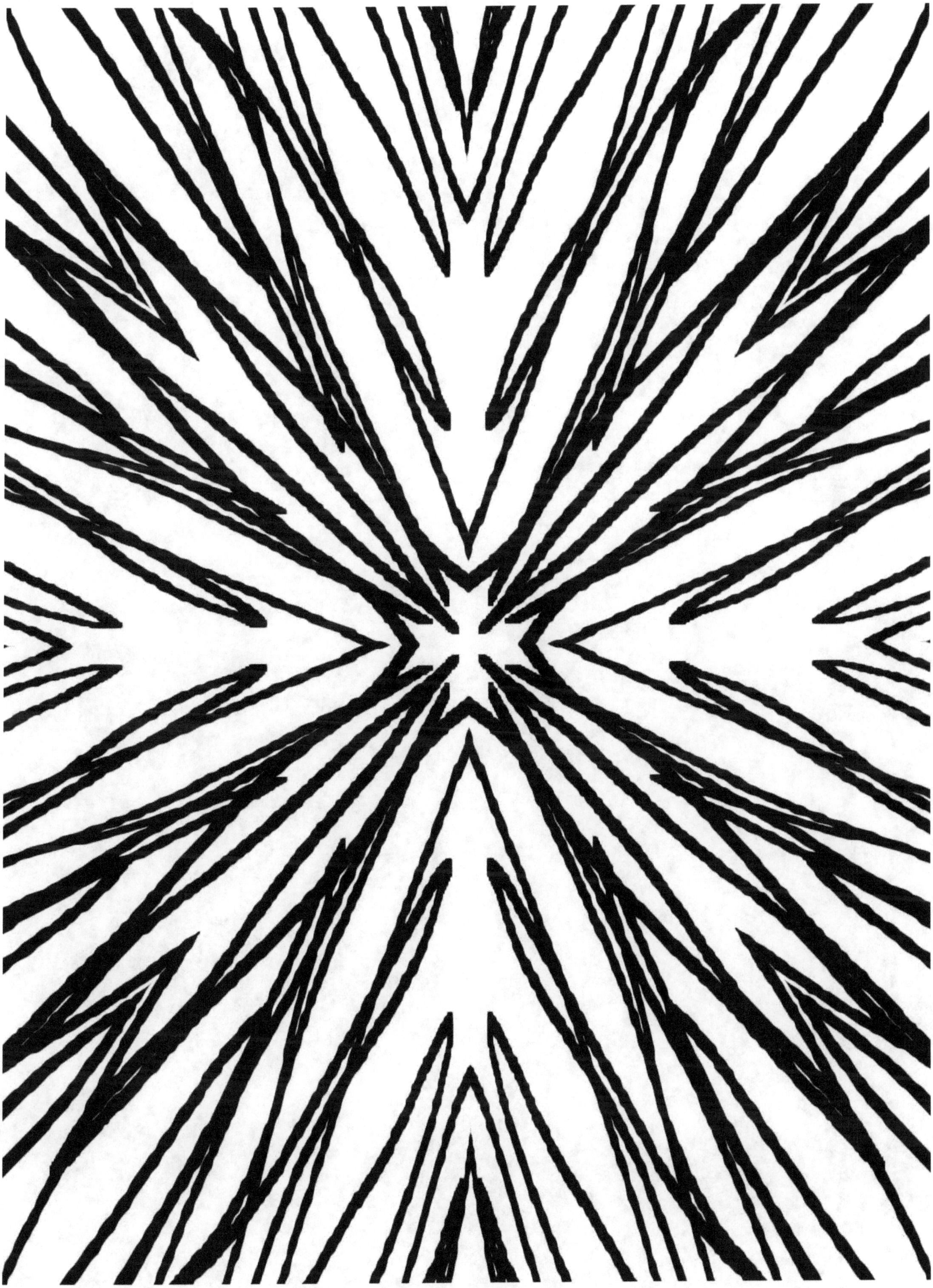

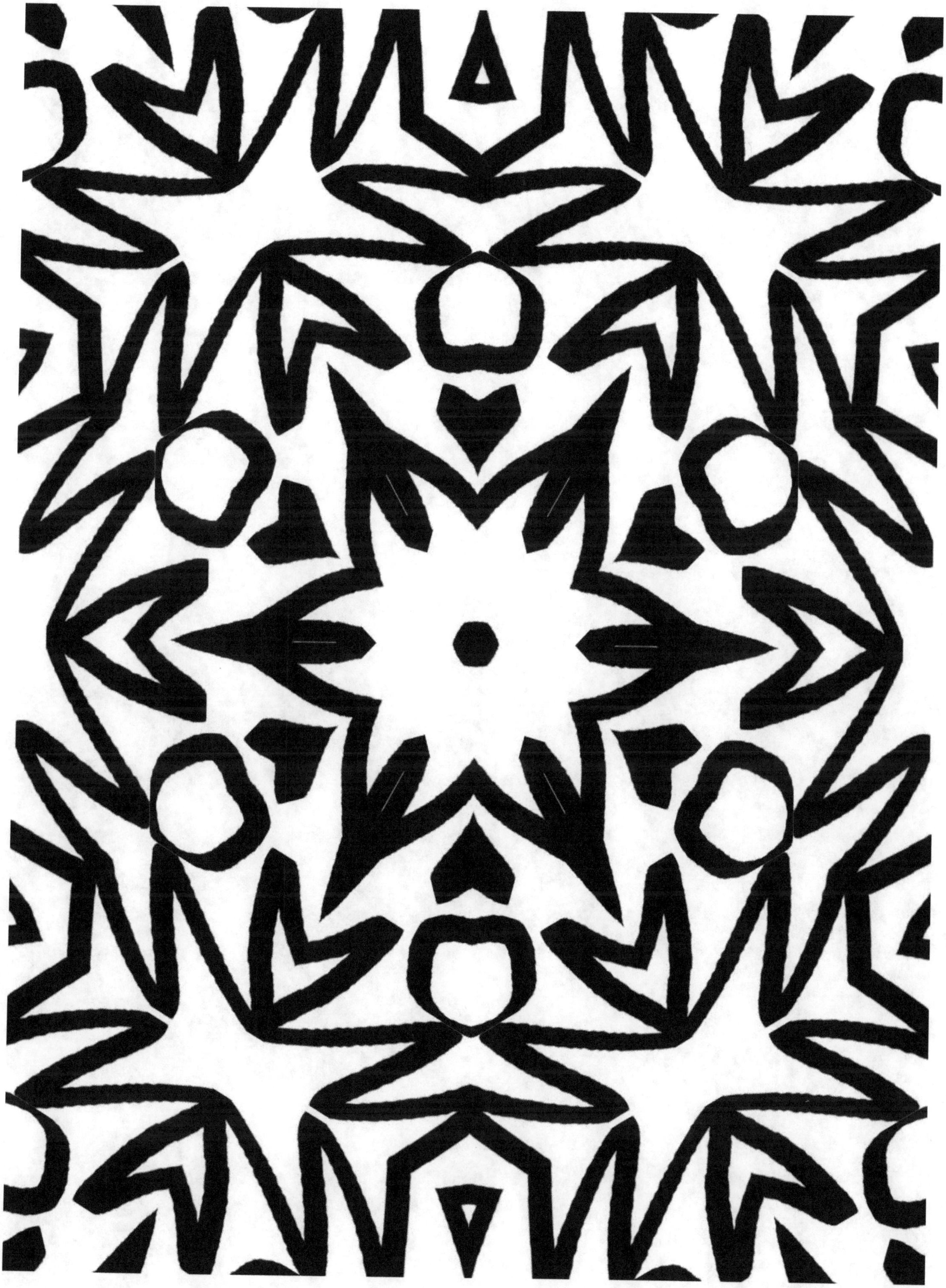

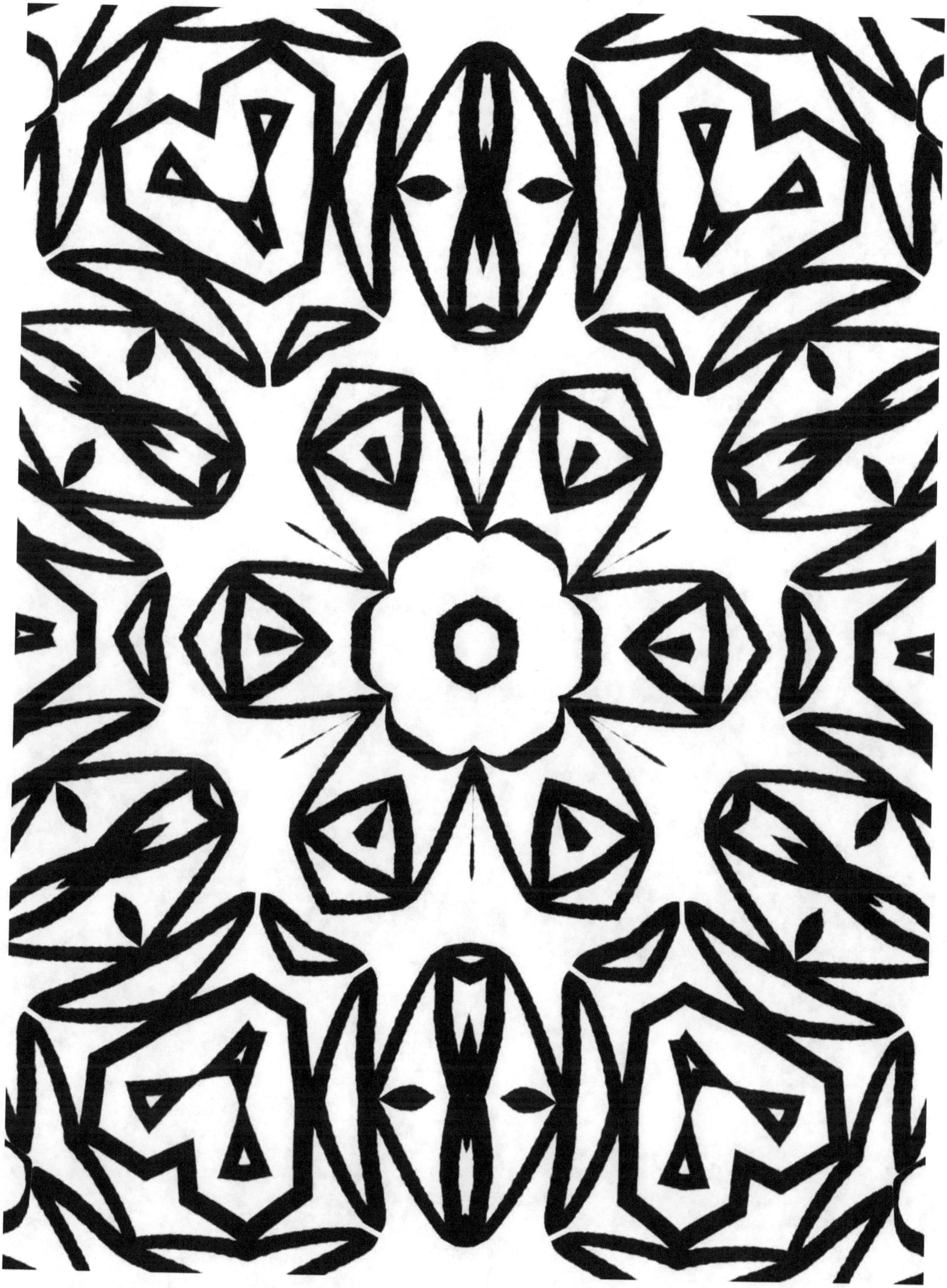

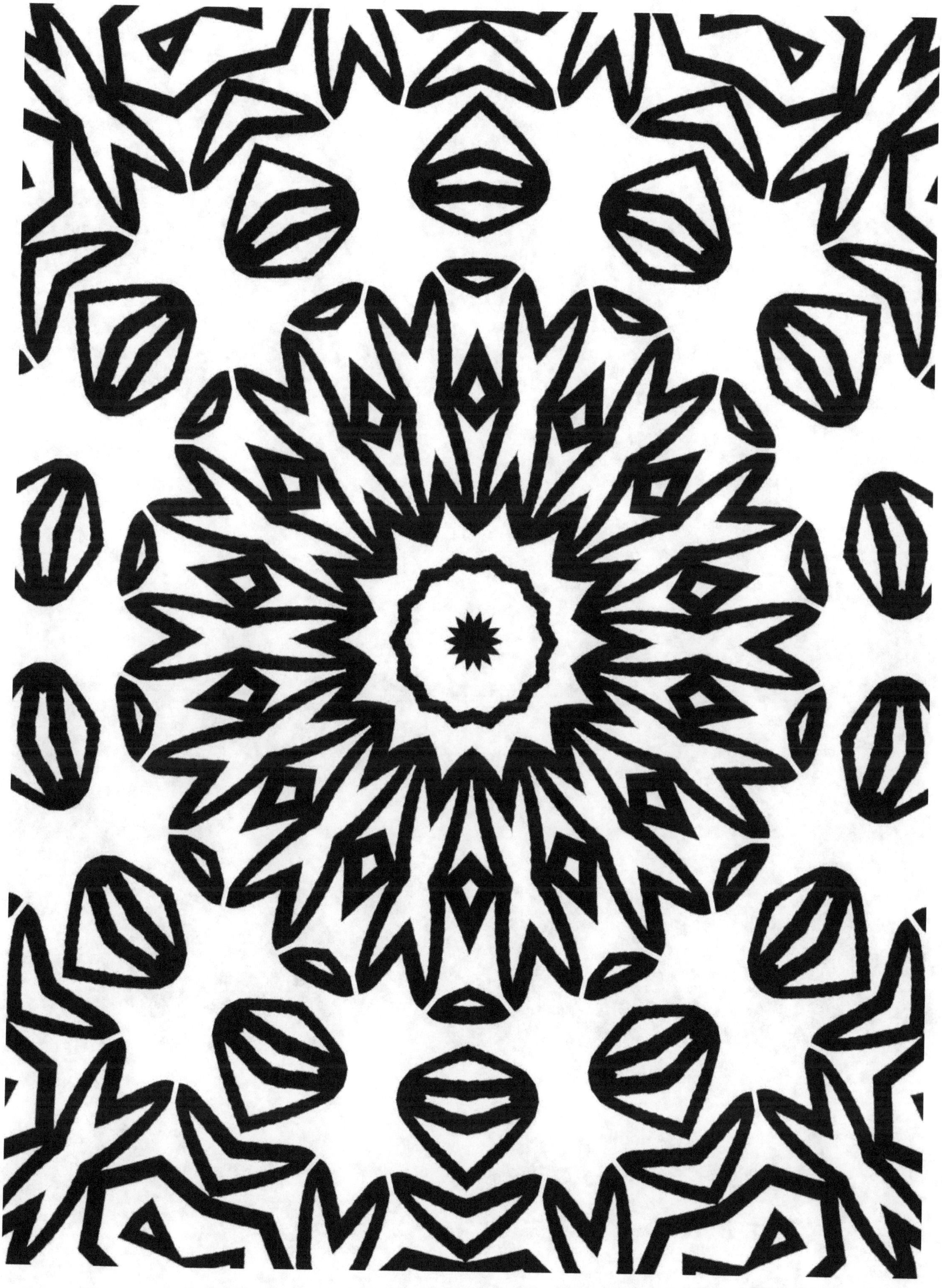

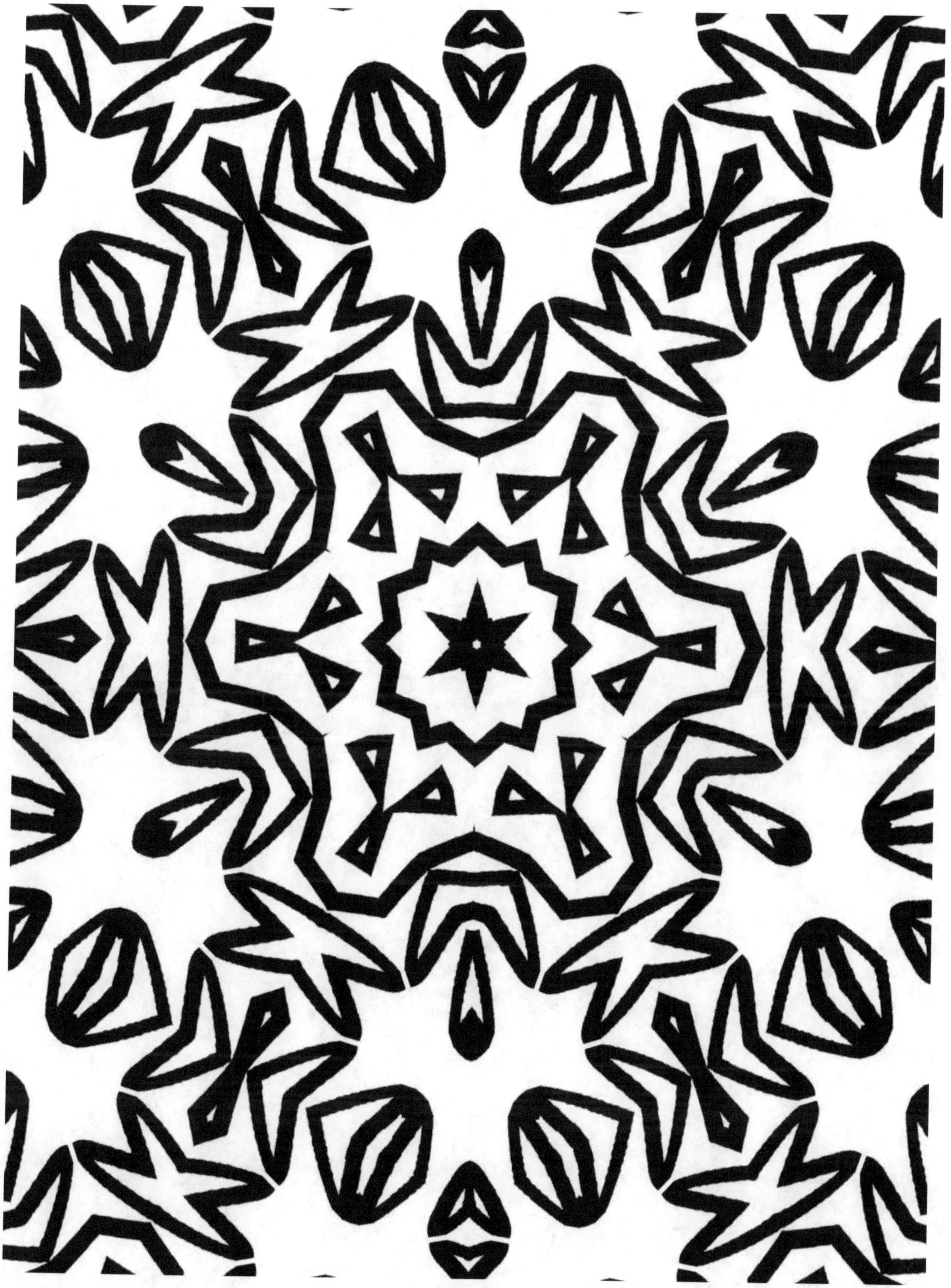

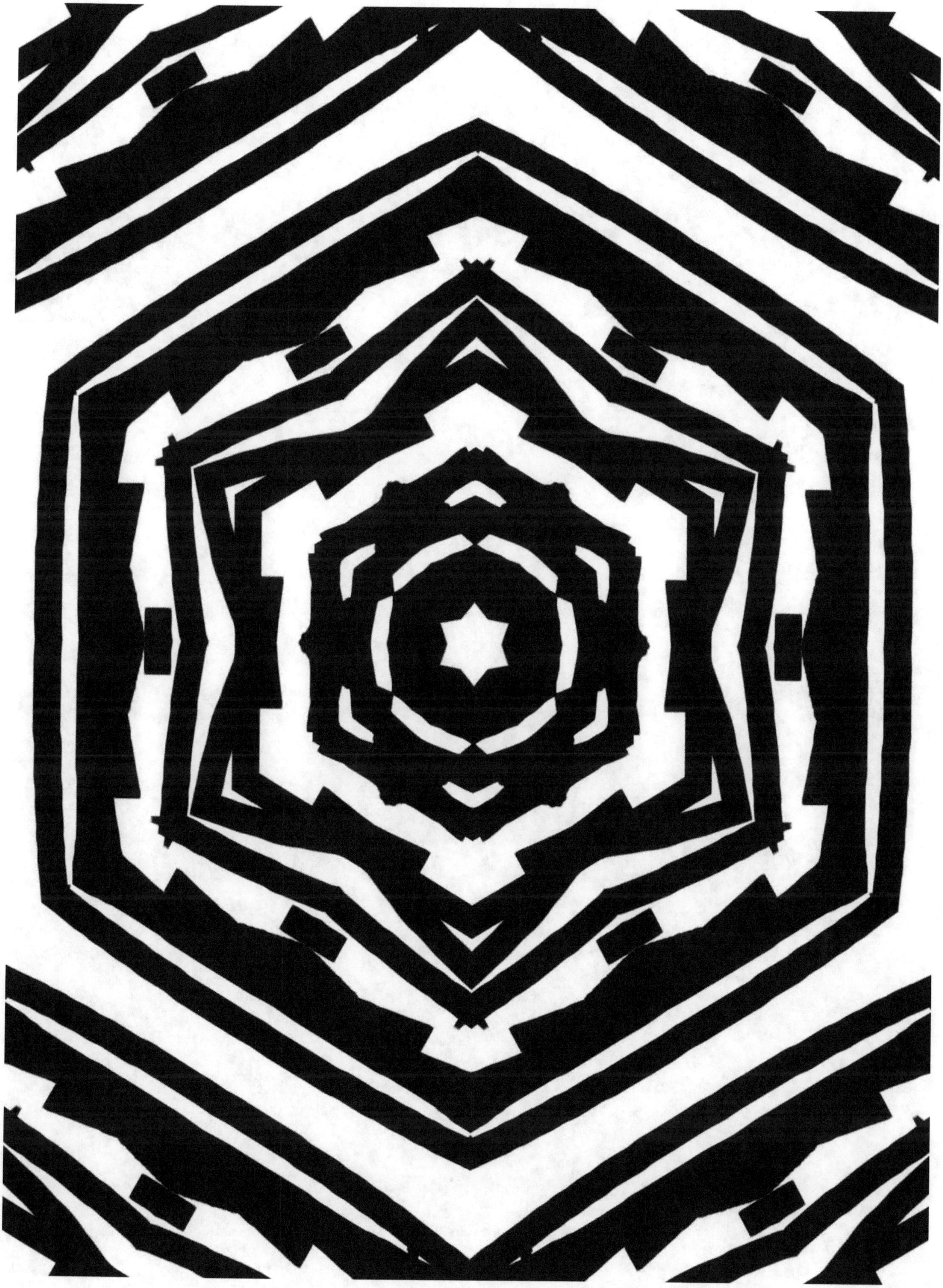

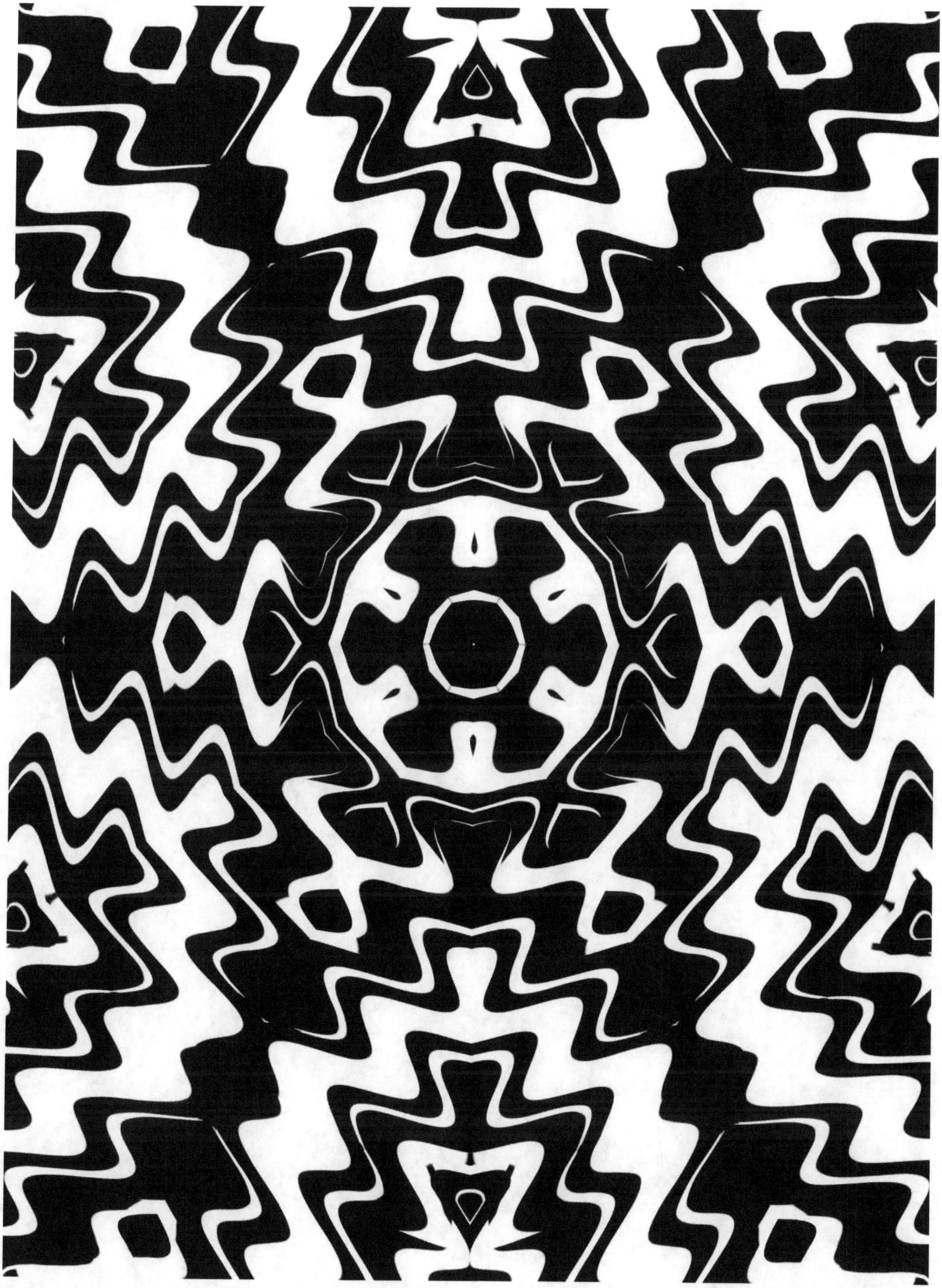

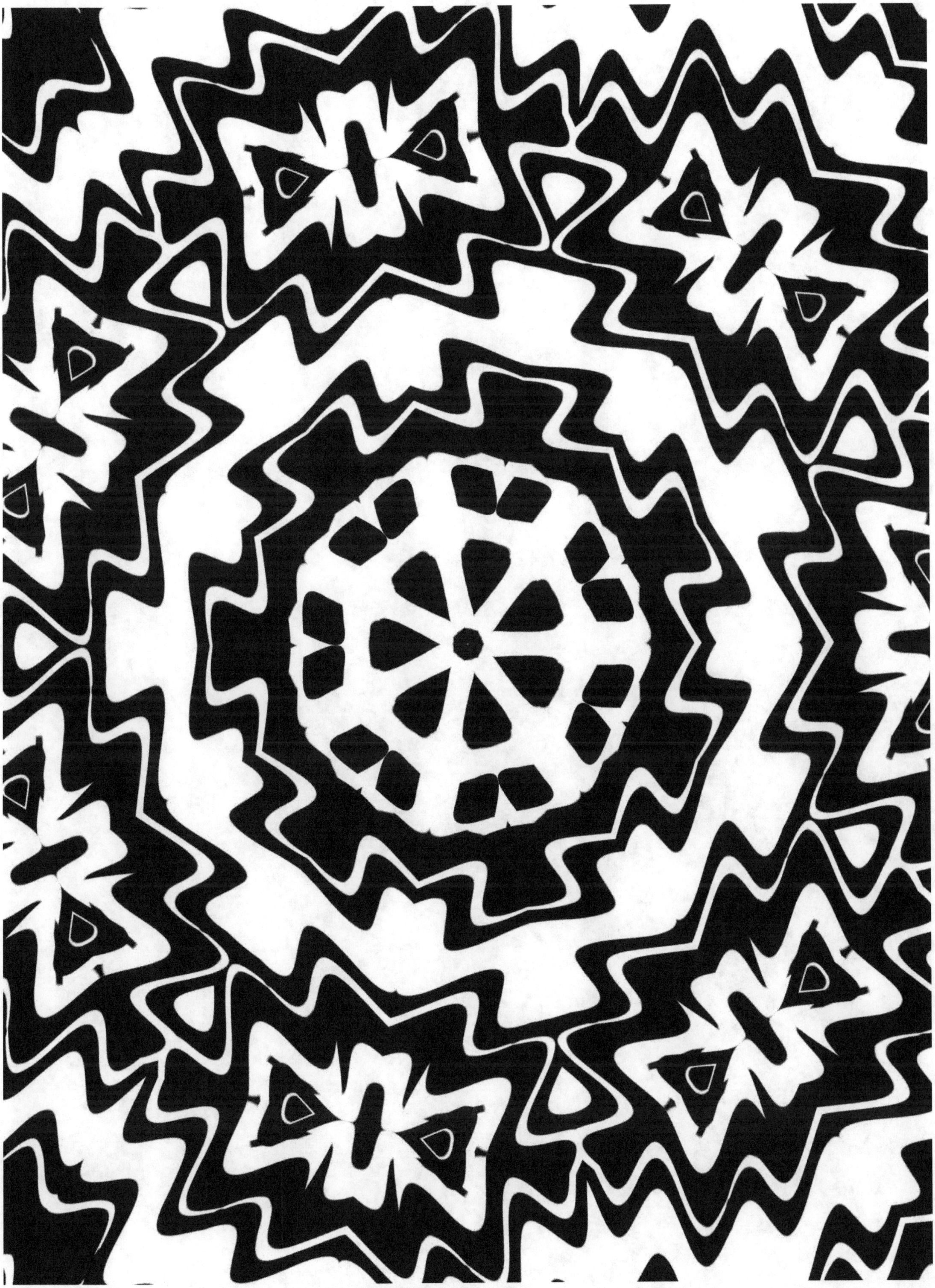

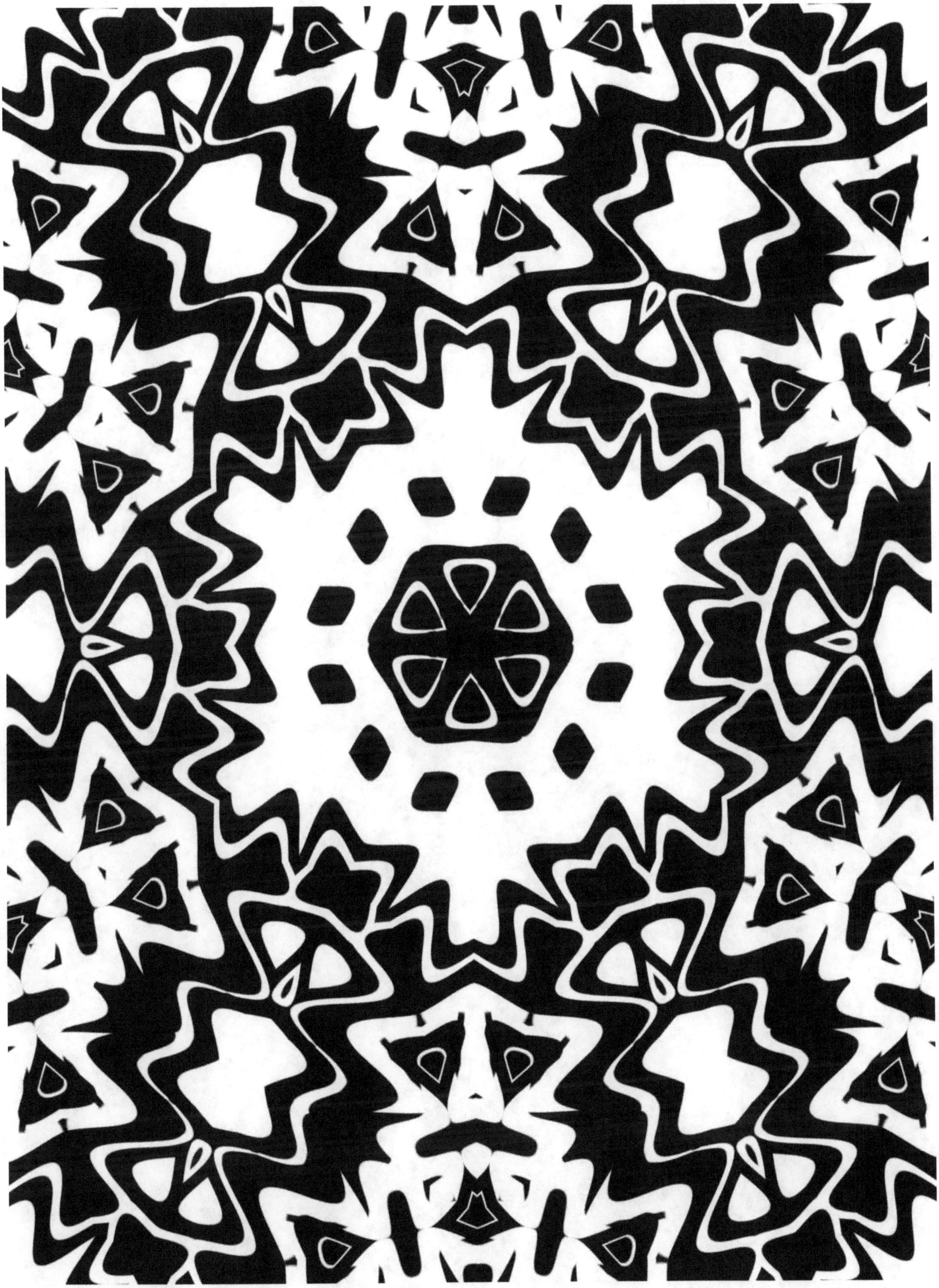

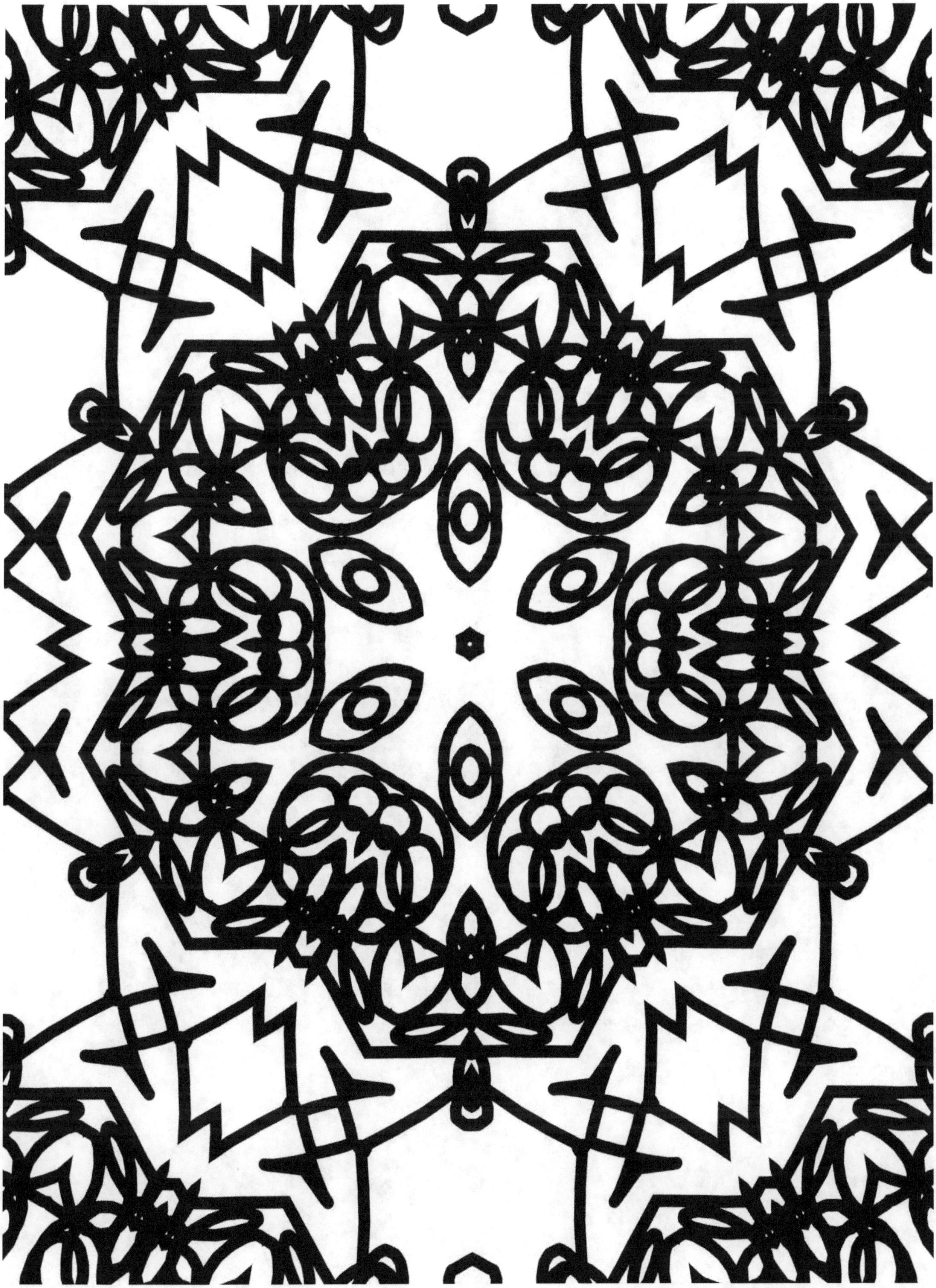

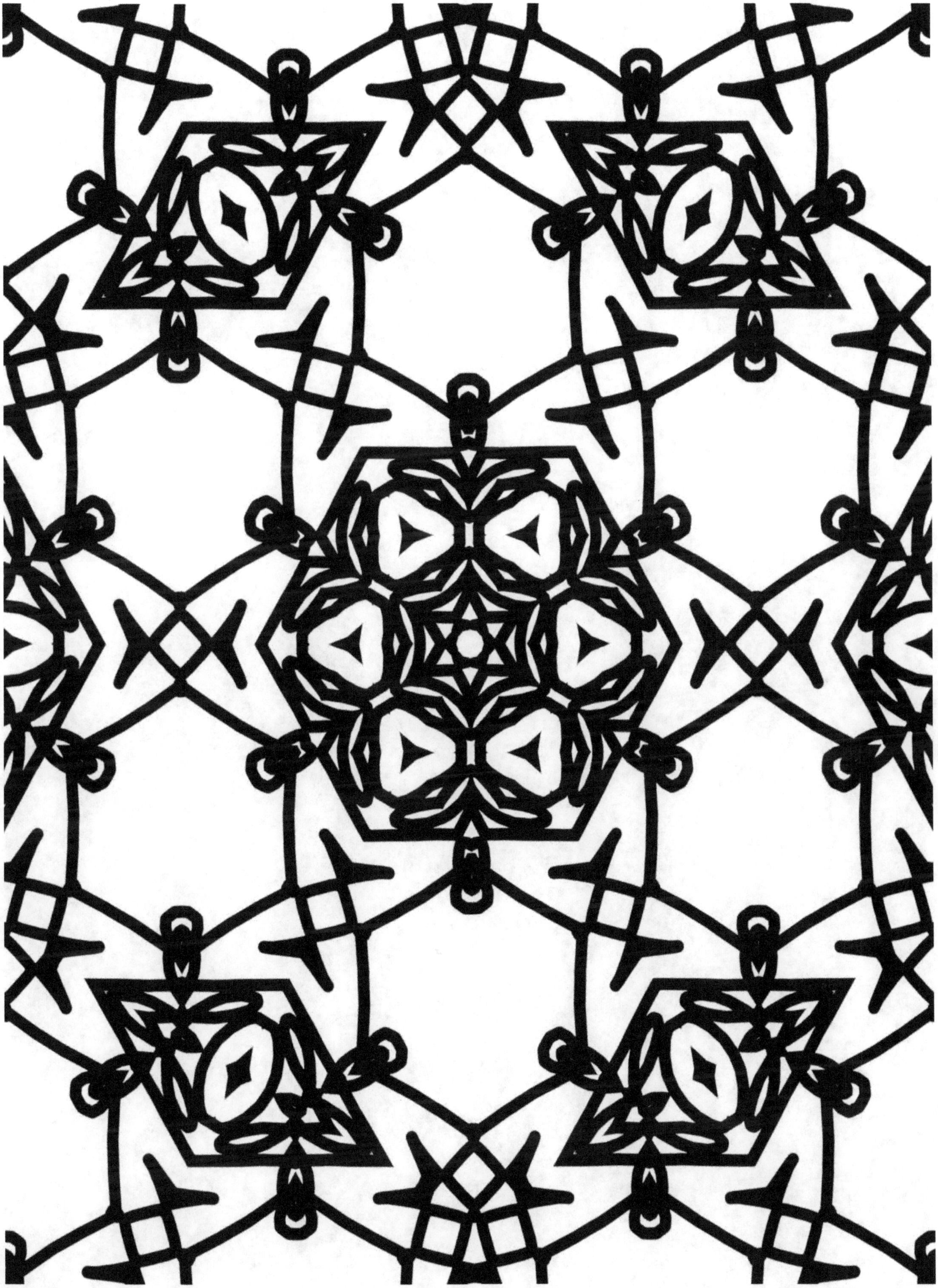

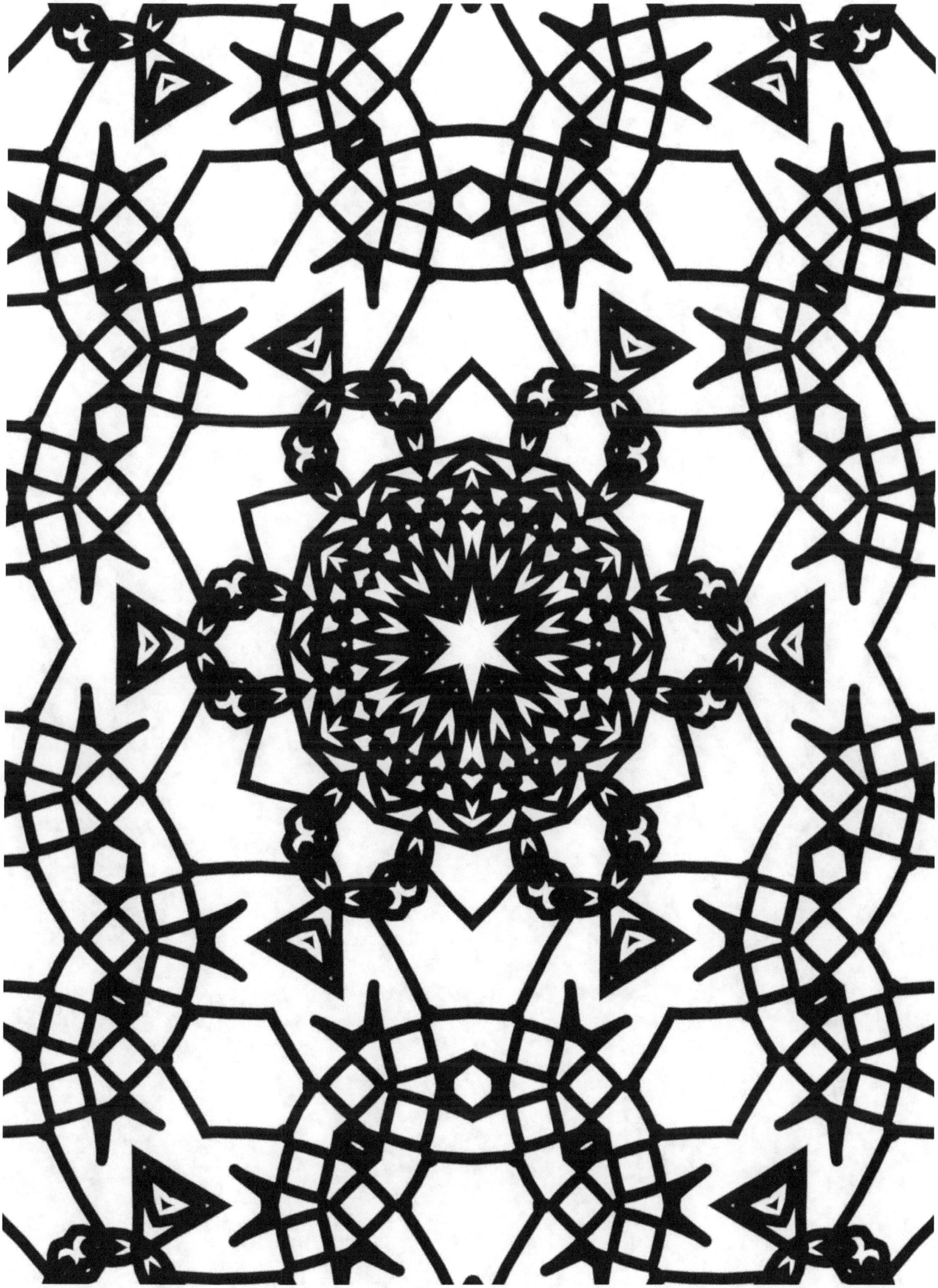

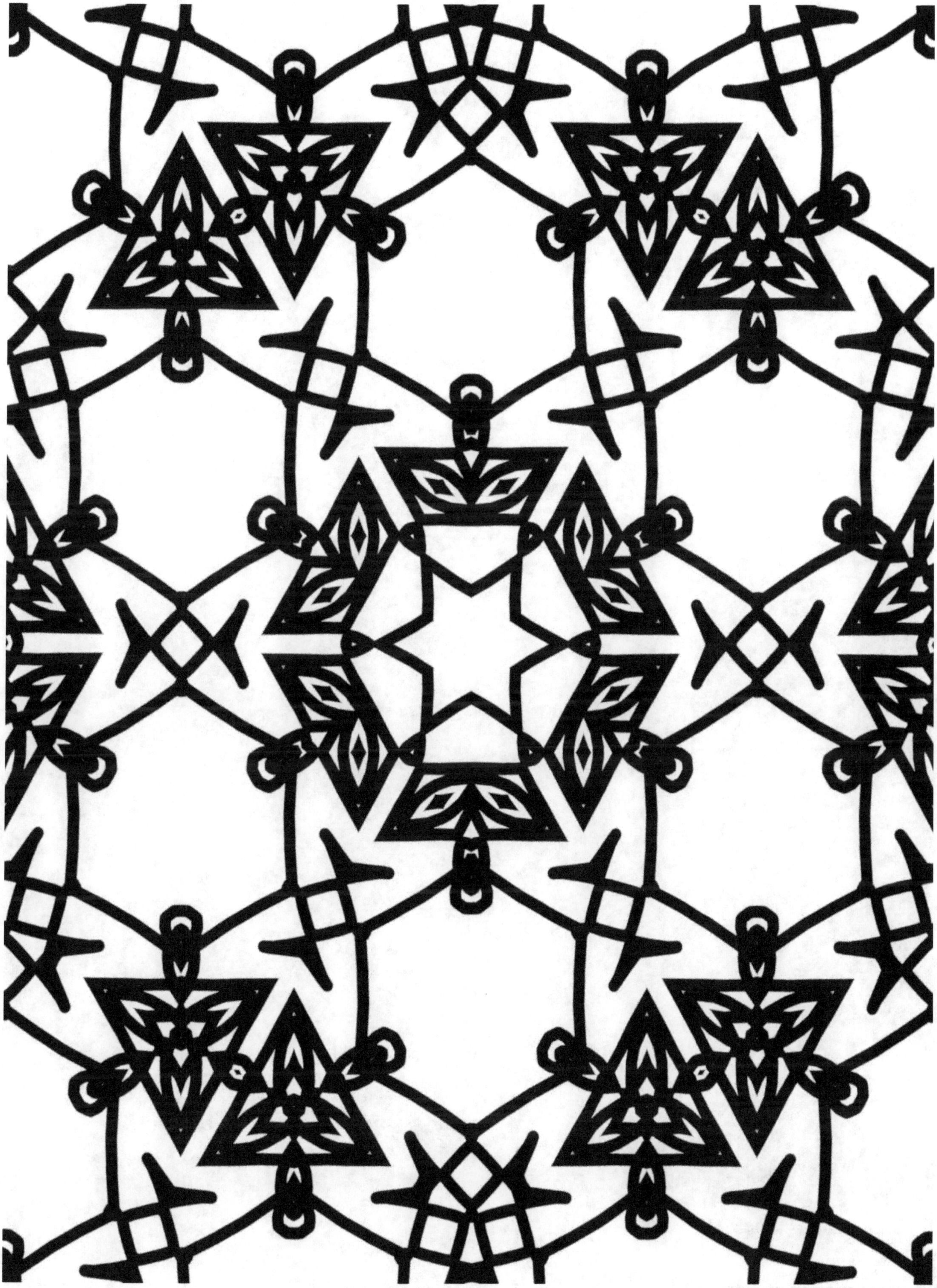

www.ingramcontent.com/pod-product-compliance
Lightning Source LLC
Chambersburg PA
CBHW080846170526
45158CB00009B/2654